PiXZ PEOPLE
Little Books of Great Lives

King Arthur

ROBERT DUNNING

First published in Great Britain in 2010

Copyright text © 2010 Robert Dunning.
Photographs:

All rights reserved. No part of this publication may be reproduced, stored in a retrieval system, or transmitted in any form or by any means without the prior permission of the copyright holder.

British Library Cataloguing-in-Publication Data
A CIP record for this title is available from the British Library

ISBN 978 1 906887 98 8

PiXZ Books
Halsgrove House, Ryelands Industrial Estate,
Bagley Road, Wellington, Somerset TA21 9PZ
Tel: 01823 653777
Fax: 01823 216796
email: sales@halsgrove.com

An imprint of Halstar Ltd, part of the Halsgrove group of companies
Information on all Halsgrove titles is available at: www.halsgrove.com

Printed and bound in China by Topan Leefung Printing Ltd

Contents

Introduction	5
One of the Nine Worthies	9
The Malory Version	13
A Hero for His Time	23
A Twelfth-Century Tale	25
Is There Truth Behind the Tale?	33
The Tale Made Taller?	37
Royal Attraction	47
Ignored By Shakespeare	51
The Return of Romance	57
Further Reading	63

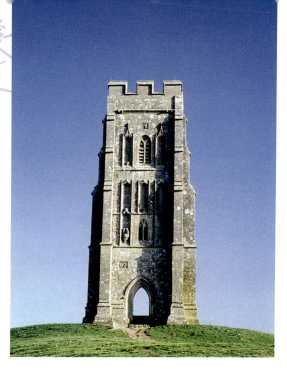

Introduction

King Arthur needs no introduction, but this little book requires one. It is an attempt, not to argue his existence but to offer, first, a sort of royal biography drawn from the man sources historians have used, beginning with Malory inn the 15th century and reaching back to Gildas in the 6th; second to record how and why English monarchs from the time of Henry II have looked to Arthur for their own political purposes; and third, to trace his regular rebirth from Malory's time to the present.

Arthur has, in fact, figured in polemical or political writing from the very beginning: from Gildas deploring the behaviour of the leaders of his own day, through the Welsh nationalism of the 9th and the 10th centuries, and the special personal pleading of Geoffrey of Monmouth for a Cornish connection, to the disintegration of government in Lancastrian England in which Malory was intimately involved.

Henry VIII saw the Round Table as an instrument of political propaganda for his European ambitions, faced with two monarchs whose ancestry made his own family origins extremely modest. Subsequent monarchs seem to have shown no particular interest in the story, but Queen Victoria chose the name Arthur for her third son in 1850 and the name was also given to her great grandson, later George VI and in 1948 to his first grandson, the present Prince of Wales.

Malory's story is, of course, hardly a history; overwhelmingly it is a series of romances that King Arthur opens and closes and otherwise plays a walk-on part. Romance in the medieval

sense has played an important part in the regular revivals of interest from the 16th century onwards. In the 17th century he was overshadowed by political and religious conflicts, but the burgeoning of interest in the medieval past of the later 18th and the 19th centuries gave a stimulus to poets and artists as well as a challenge to historians. The 20th century perhaps saw the story as an escape from the consequences of two world wars, and the court of Camelot was transferred in the minds of some to the White House in Washington.

For historians, the story will always be a matter of controversy. That, in itself, keeps King Arthur very much alive.

> *I think both sides are to blame about him; I mean those who tell Incredible Tales of him, such as are utterly inconsistent with the circumstances of the British at that time, and those who deny that there was any such person, or of any considerable power, among the Britons.*
> Edward Stillingfleet, Bishop of Worcester, 1699

One of the Nine Worthies

For generations, educated people agreed that there had been nine outstanding men in the world's history. Three came from the Classical World: Hector of Troy, Alexander the Great and Julius Caesar; three from Biblical times: Joshua, David and Judas Maccabaeus; and three from the Christian world: King Arthur, Charlemagne, Emperor of the Franks, and Godfrey de Bouillon, Ruler of Jerusalem after the First Crusade. Many of those famous nine have long been forgotten but King Arthur is a name recognised still by old and young around the world, for many a figure associated with chivalry and romance. But for many he is controversial, sometimes dismissed as pure fiction, sometimes the embodiment of some ancient truth. Real or not, the influence of his story was profound for much of the Middle Ages and in more modern times it has inspired words and pictures and music that are at the heart of our culture.

The famous printer William Caxton, when asked by King Edward IV to produce a book on King Arthur as part of the continuing revival of Arthurian interest that had been a mark of his reign, was at first uncertain about the idea, arguing that, in contrast to the other Worthies, Arthur was a fictional character, his story 'feigned and fables'. Yet eventually he was persuaded because, as he wrote, people regularly visited Arthur's tomb at Glastonbury, saw his seal at Westminster, the amazing earthworks at Caerleon, the Round Table at Winchester, Gawain's skull and Craddock's mantle at Dover Castle, and Lancelot's sword. Many people, too, had read the history of the king and his knights as told by Geoffrey of Monmouth, Chretien de Troyes and by many others in most European languages.

King Arthur stands between Godfrey de Bouillon and Charlemagne in a 15th-century German tapestry.

So Caxton put aside his doubts and agreed. Adapting an English translation of stories in French completed in 1469-70 by Sir Thomas Malory, he produced in 1485 the first printed version of a book that has had the most enormous effect in the English-speaking world ever since.

The book Caxton printed is not a single story but 507 chapters with two main themes: the reign of King Arthur which begins with hope and ends in catastrophe; and the Quest for the Holy Grail involving Lancelot, Galahad and others. Malory had called his work 'The Hoole Booke of Kyng Arthur and of his Noble Knyghtes of the Rounde Table'; Caxton chose the rather less accurate *Le Morte Darthur* - 'The Death of Arthur'.

Bedevere bids farewell to Excalibur at the lake. Aubrey Beardsley

> *So many scholars have spent so much time trying to establish whether Arthur existed at all that they have lost track of the single truth that he exists over and over.*
> John Steinbeck

The opening page of William Caxton's edition of Sir Thomas Malory's Le Morte D'Arthur.

The Malory Version

Arthur's father was Uther Pendragon, king of all England, his mother Igraine, wife of Gorlois and Uther's enemy. Her seduction at Tintagel was arranged by the wizard Merlin who made Uther appear to Igraine as her husband Gorlois; but Gorlois himself was killed a few hours before the meeting actually took place. Uther married Igraine but Merlin arranged that the resulting child was brought up as the son of a knight named Ector.

Long uncertainty following the death of Uther was brought to an end when Merlin advised the archbishop of Canterbury to summon all the lords and gentlemen of arms by Christmas to London. There they gathered in the city's greatest church and after much prayer, a stone appeared in its churchyard 'four square, like unto a marble stone, and in the midst thereof was like an anvil of steel a foot on high, and therein stuck a fair

Previous page: *Arthur removes the sword from the anvil, offers it at the altar and is crowned. Flemish, about 1290.*

The headland at Tintagel, Cornwall.

sword naked by the point'. Around the sword were letters written in gold: 'Whoso pulleth out this sword of this stone and anvil, is rightwise king born of all England'.

On New Year's Day, after more prayers, jousting and tournaments were organised 'for to keep the lords and the commons together'. Arthur, acting as squire to Sir Ector's son Kay, in complete innocence pulled the sword from the stone to save returning to their lodgings to fetch another as he had been instructed. Kay recognised the sword and took it to his father who, suspecting the truth, asked Arthur to put it back in the stone. Kay 'pulled at the sword with all his might, but it would not be', while in his turn Arthur pulled it out easily. Ector and Kay thus recognised Arthur as their lord and reported their story to the archbishop. The lords were summoned on Twelfth Day, again at Candlemas and again at Easter, but none but Arthur could move the sword. Then on Merlin's advice Arthur was protected by several of King Uther's most trusted knights until Pentecost when the lords tried again without success. Finally the commons cried at once 'We will have Arthur unto our king ... and who that holdith against it, we will slay him'.

So Arthur offered the sword to the archbishop at the altar, was knighted and crowned. Lands taken from their rightful owners since King Uther's death were returned, the 'countries' around London were 'stablished', and the officers of state were appointed: Sir Kay as seneschal, Sir Baudwin of Britain constable, Sir Ulfius chamberlain, Sir Brastias warden 'to wait upon the north from the Trent forwards' and later Lucas the butler.

At Pentecost a year after his coronation, Arthur announced a great feast at Caerleon. King Lot of Lothian and of Orkney, King Uriens of Gore, King Nentres of Garlot, the king of Scotland, the king of Carados, and an unnamed king arrived with large retinues, but rejected the presents Arthur offered as 'gifts of a beardless boy that was come of low blood' and instead threatened to kill him. Arthur retreated to a 'strong tower' with five hundred men and the kings laid siege

to it. Merlin arrived after some days, was unable to convince all the kings, but persuaded Arthur to come out and explain himself. The parley produced no agreement and Arthur returned to the tower where his men armed themselves to fight. Merlin advised him not to use the sword he 'had by miracle', the sword Excalibur, until the fight began to go against him.

Arthur had a horse killed under him but Excalibur was 'so bright in his enemies' eyes, that it gave light like thirty torches. The kings were put to flight and 'much people' were killed, the 'commons' of Caerleon joining in with clubs and staves.

At a council in London the barons did not know how to prevent such a revolt again but by the advice of Merlin Arthur proposed to ask for the help of King Ban of Benwick and King Bors of

The coronation of Arthur, probably by Matthew Paris, 1230-50.

Gaul. In return he promised to help them both in their quarrel with King Claudas. Ban and Bors agreed, and Merlin brought ten thousand of their men to the forest of Bedegraine. Arthur brought a similar number to Bedegraine castle.

Meanwhile the six kings found allies: the duke of Cambenet, King Brandegoris of Stranggore, King Clariance of Northumberland, King Ydres of Cornwall, King Cradlemas or Cradlement of North Wales and King Agwisance of Ireland, each with large retinues. Malory took four chapters to describe the horrific details of the battle that followed in which so many died.

At last, Merlin called a halt to the fighting, telling Arthur that the eleven kings needed to withdraw because their lands had been invaded by Saracens. Arthur could thus go and help his friend King Leodegrance of Cameliard fight off King Rience of North Wales.

After such fighting the youth had become a man, but the secrecy surrounding his conception and his complete ignorance of his own origins brought complications that eventually proved fatal. He had a child by Lionors who was named Borre and became a member of the Round Table, and a son, Mordred, by Morgawse, the wife of his enemy King Lot of Orkney, who quite unknown to him was his half-sister. Mordred survived a Massacre of the Innocents ordered by Arthur and lived to destroy him. Arthur married Guinevere, daughter of Leodegrance, in spite of Merlin's warning that she would be unfaithful with Lancelot. With her came the Round Table that had once belonged to Uther Pendragon. His mother Igraine was accused of treason by those who did not know the circumstances of Arthur's birth; and another of Igraine's daughters, Morgan le Fay, wife of King Uriens, attempted to kill Arthur as well as her own husband.

There were still those who challenged the king. First came messengers from the Emperor of Rome demanding a tax as a mark of his supremacy, then another messenger from King Rience saying that he had 'discomfited and overcome' eleven kings, who in acknowledgement gave him their beards which he fixed to his mantle. He now demanded Arthur's beard to complete the set. The twelve kings who had earlier challenged Arthur, including Lot, were eventually overcome and were buried honourably at Camelot, but Arthur had then to face an invasion by the king of Denmark, his brother the king of Ireland, and the kings of the Vale, Soleise and the Isle of Longtains. Those five were killed by Arthur, Kay, Griflet and Gawain near the Humber and some thirty thousand of their men fell. Arthur founded the abbey of La Beale Adventure on the battle site.

The greatest challenge came from the Emperor Lucius, demanding tribute as successor to Julius Caesar. So a great army was gathered including the kings of Scotland and Little Britain and the lord of West Wales with Uwaine, Ider and Lancelot. Lucius, with an army gathered from the whole empire, crossed the Alps and reached Cologne and summoned troops to Burgundy. Arthur, meanwhile, after holding a parliament at York and appointing two governors of the realm in his absence, sailed from Sandwich. At a great battle in the vale of Sessoine the emperor, the sultan of Syria and the kings of Egypt and Ethiopia were killed and their bodies sent to Rome as sufficient tribute from Britain, Ireland and all Almaine with Germany. Arthur then made his way to Rome via 'Loraine, Brabant and Flanders … Haut Almaine … Lombardy … Tuscany … Spolute and Viterbe' and was crowned emperor by the pope.

The story of the successful ruler, king become emperor, is now almost done; but Malory has more tales to tell, notably the search for the Holy Grail. Mark, Tristram, Percivale, Gawaine and the rest joust, quarrel, encounter maidens and occasionally return to court and the Round Table and to a king who seems little more than a shadow. After many chapters, the political story resumes when Agravaine and Mordred reveal the affair between Lancelot and Guinevere.

The king's nephews Gareth and Gaheris were killed in an attempt to capture Lancelot. Lancelot, supported by Bors and Lionel, faced Arthur outside Lancelot's castle of Joyous Gard, perhaps Alnwick or Bamburgh, where he held the queen. A

Alnwick castle, Northumberland.

Bamburgh castle, Northumberland.

battle followed in which many were killed. The pope intervened through the bishop of Rochester. Lancelot was given a safe conduct (opposed by Gawaine) and Guinevere returned to the king at Carlisle. Lancelot and his followers left Cardiff for his lands in Benwick — Beaune or Bayonne were alternative names — and he became overlord of the whole of France.

Arthur and Gawaine made war upon him there, but news came that Mordred, reporting that Arthur had been killed, had persuaded the lords of parliament to make him king. He had already been crowned at Canterbury, and planned to make Guinevere his queen. Arthur and Gawain landed at Dover and in a battle there Gawaine was killed. Another battle, somewhere between Salisbury and the sea, ended as each gave the other a fatal blow. Mordred died immediately, Arthur was taken away by boat by three queens but was later buried in a chapel at Glastonbury. Bedivere, on the king's orders, reluctantly threw the king's sword Excalibur into the sea. Lancelot, ashamed of his behaviour, returned and became a priest, Guinevere a nun at Ambresbury. Constantine of Cornwall became king of Britain.

> That ancient, worthy king of the Britons, in whose acts there is truth enough to make him famous, besides that which is fabulous.
> Francis Bacon, *History of Henry VII*

Overleaf: The dying Arthur taken by three queens to the Isle of Avalon. Daniel Maclise, 1893

A Hero for His Time

So Malory. Some took the story as history, some as pure fiction. The political intrigues he described were not at all unlike those of his own day, in which he was actively involved though he spent much time in prison: the struggles of the Wars of the Roses included the choice of a king by parliament, just as Mordred was chosen while Arthur was still alive, and events were often influenced by 'the commons'. The use of names of places like London, Westminster, Winchester, York, and Dover suggest authenticity, exactly the places where the significant events of his lifetime took place. And his knights wore fashionable armour and wielded the latest weapons. Yet their quests, their jousting, their romancing were of an age long past and of a country not his own. His sources were 'French books', as he declared quite openly. He was no historian; he was, as John Steinbeck once remarked, a novelist who had plenty of time while in prison

York.

to develop his own style and not be encumbered with research.

So, as his French sources suggested, he told stories of an earlier age and culture: knights on adventures rescuing damsels in distress, hermits, dwarves, magic swords, enchanted forests, dreams, love potions, and the story of Galahad, the purest knight in the world, the only man to reach the Holy Grail. And in between, days of feasting and friendly jousting leading to serious wounds, jealousy to bitter quarrels, murders, vengeance and open rebellion. And Arthur himself always in the background but not actively involved, ruling his realm, presiding over his court but allowing events to take their course without any direction from him. A king without power.

But Malory's sources must have included a work by his time three centuries old and well known. In 1135, the Welshman Geoffrey of Monmouth, as part of a book entitled *Historia Regum Britanniae* (History of the Kings of Britain), told the story of King Arthur without the romantic embellishments in a way that convinced his many readers that he was a great military leader of the Dark Ages.

> *As a person Malory's Arthur is a fool. As a legend he is timeless. You can't explain him in human terms any more than you can explain Jesus.*
> John Steinbeck.

A Twelfth-Century Tale

Arthur was the son of Uther Pendragon, king of Britain, by Ygerna, the wife of Gorlois, duke of Cornwall. He was conceived, thanks to help from Merlin, at Tintagel while her husband was being besieged at Dimilioc not far away. There Gorlois was killed, Uther and Ygerna 'lived together as equals, united by their great love for each other' and had a son and a daughter, Arthur and Anna. Anna married Loth of Lodonesia and by him had two sons, Gawaine and Mordred.

In the later years of King Uther's reign his kingdom suffered attacks from the Saxons and he won a last victory against them at St Albans but afterwards was poisoned by Saxon spies. Dubricius, archbishop of the City of the Legions [Caerleon], in face of renewed attacks by the Saxons, summoned the British leaders to Silchester so that Arthur might be crowned. He was then only fifteen years old. As king he led his people towards York, won a victory beside the River Douglas, and surrounded the survivors in the city. A further invasion from Germany was imminent and Arthur retired to London, seeking help from his cousin King Hoel of Brittany. The combined army then

The headland at Tintagel, Cornwall.

Roman foundations, St Albans.

marched on Lincoln and destroyed the Saxons, who were pursued to Caledon Wood, where he forced them to agree to leave the country. They broke their agreement, however, and landed on the coast near Totnes, wreaking havoc across the countryside as far as the Severn and laid siege to Bath. Arthur, who had begun to harass the Scots and the Picts, left Hoel behind in Alclud and made for Somerset.

After Archbishop Dubricius in effect made the forthcoming fight a Christian crusade, Arthur put on a golden helmet topped with a dragon crest, a shield called Pridwen with the image of the Virgin, his sword Caliburn that had been forged in the Isle of Avalon and his spear called Ron. A fierce battle followed, with Arthur attacking the Saxon hilltop position. They were eventually defeated and while Cador, duke of Cornwall, pursued the survivors to Thanet, Arthur himself returned to Albany to rescue Hoel at Alculd, driving the Picts and Scots to Moray and then Loch Lomond. An attempt by King Gilmaurius of Ireland to support them was brushed aside, but eventually Arthur was persuaded by Scots bishops to stop fighting and grant pardon.

The king then moved to York for Christmas, shocked at the devastation the Saxons had left behind. All was restored and the former British rulers were reinstated, Auguselus became king of the Scots, his brother Urien ruler of Moray, and Loth, Arthur's brother-in-law, duke of Lothian. The king himself then married Guinevere, descendant of a noble Roman family and

Bath.

A busy street in York.

'the most beautiful woman in the entire island'. In the following summer Arthur invaded and conquered Ireland and Iceland, and in face of such power the kings of Gotland and of the Orkneys promised him tribute.

For the next twelve years there was peace and Arthur 'developed ... a code of courtliness in his household', though the king's world-wide fame aroused both fear and jealousy.

So Arthur turned his attention to Norway, supporting his brother-in-law Loth in a lawful claim to the crown. Then he moved to Gaul, which he won in single combat outside Paris with the Tribune Frollo, who ruled on behalf of the Emperor Leo. All France fell under his control, and he gave parts of it to his faithful followers: Bedevere ruled Normandy, Kay Anjou. A further nine years passed, and at a Whitsun crown-wearing ceremony at Caerleon the king summoned all who owed him homage.

Caerleon was a fine city of gold-roofed palaces, a nunnery, a monastery that was the seat of an archbishop, and a large *college specialising in astronomy and other arts. There came the tribute kings from Cornwall, North and South Wales, Scotland and Moray; the archbishops of London and York, and of course Dubricius himself, the Primate of Britain and Papal Legate. British earls came from Gloucester, Worcester, Salisbury, Warwick, Leicester, Caistor, Bath, Dorchester and Oxford. And then, more remarkable still, were leaders from further afield: Ireland, Iceland, Gotland, the Orkneys, Norway and Denmark, Hoiland, Normandy, Anjou, Poitou, Gaul and Hoel, the leader of the Armorican Britons.*

Such a display of power was too much of a challenge for the Emperor Lucius to ignore, so he summoned Arthur to his court for behaviour he described as insolent and threatened to invade Britain. Arthur and his allies gathered a massive army. In his turn the emperor gathered a huge force from Spain, Africa, Greece, Babylon and the Orient.

Arthur left Britain with his wife Guinevere and his nephew Mordred in charge, crossing the channel from Southampton to

Le Mont St Michel.

Barfleur. After a diversion to Mont St Michel in pursuit of a giant who had kidnapped and murdered Hoel's niece, his army marched towards Autun. By the time they reach the river Aube they found the Romans were not far away. After heavy skirmishing and a Roman retreat through Langres towards Autun, the final battle was joined in a valley called Saussy. Among Arthur's close allies, Bedevere was killed and Kay mortally wounded, but victory was won by the decisive intervention of Gawaine and Hoel. Lucius himself lay dead. After some delay Arthur prepared to set our for Rome, but news of Mordred's treachery came from Britain.

In the absence of his uncle temptation had proved too great. Mordred had made himself king and was living with his uncle's wife.

Geoffrey of Monmouth apologises to his patron for making no comment on such an event, but describes the battle between the two from what he had read in the 'British treatise' he had quoted earlier and also from the historian Walter, archdeacon of Oxford.

Mordred had sent for help from the enemy Saxons in return for that part of the kingdom from the Humber to Scotland and also part of Kent the Saxons had once held. His army included disaffected Scots and Picts. Arthur landed at Richborough and in the first battle between the two sides Gawaine and the king of Albany were killed. Mordred was then driven to Winchester and when Guinevere heard she fled from York to Caerleon and there took vows as a nun. A second defeat for Mordred at Winchester was followed by his flight by sea towards Cornwall. At Camblam came the last battle in which Mordred was killed and Arthur himself was mortally wounded. He was 'carried off to the Isle of Avalon, so that his wounds might be attended to'. He handed over the crown of Britain to his cousin Constantine, son of Cador duke of Cornwall. This was in the year 542.

Slaughter Bridge, Camelford, Cornwall.

> *The amazing success of Geoffrey of Monmouth's Historia Regum Britanniae is at least as interesting as the stories it relates.* Elizabeth Jenkins
>
> *It was the hero of the losing side, King Arthur, who imposed himself on the imagination, the chief and lasting contribution of the Celts to the mind and literature of Europe.*
> A L Rowse, *The Spirit of English History*

Geoffrey of Monmouth's brilliance in creating Arthur as a figure entirely believable in his time was equalled by his second creation, Merlin. His name is Geoffrey's adaptation of the Welsh Myrddin, who in Welsh legend was a bard from North Wales who lived towards the end of the 6th century and who is said to have had the gift of prophecy and to have foretold a British revival. From a 9th-century source he created a young poet-prophet from Carmarthen who, inexplicably, oversaw the building of Stonehenge and then contrived the affair at Tintagel.

Geoffrey's new character evidently so intrigued him that about 1150 he wrote a long poem called *Vita Merlini*. From that the later romancers created the enchanter who protected the young Arthur, brought him to kingship and became in his early years his chief adviser.

> *Sir King, there be but two old men that know:*
> *… and one*
> *is Merlin, the wise man that ever served*
> *King Uther thro' his magic art*
> *… and whatsoever Merlin did*
> *In one great annal-book, where after-years*
> *Will learn the secret of or Arthur's birth*
> A Tennyson, *The Coming of Arthur*

Is There Truth Behind the Tale?

So Geoffrey of Monmouth provides a precise date, and a reasonable one if the story belongs to the Dark Ages when Britain was indeed being invaded by the Saxons. And sources cited in support sound reasonable: British treatises and the opinion of Walter the archdeacon, historian. In comparison with Malory this seems serious history. Noble knights named Kay, Bedevere and Gawaine are included, but no courtly love save one chance use of the word 'courtliness'. No Lancelot, no Galahad, no Grail, not much magic, a giant and a dream or two; but victor (clearly often only possible with cavalry, which might feel more like the 12th century than the 6th) in great battles against invading Saxons, one near Bath. Then he became an aggressive empire builder and finally challenger of Rome. A fine if inherently fanciful description of Caerleon, but other identifiable place-names in abundance. And here was the introduction of Avalon where the king's spear was made and where his wounds were attended to. And significant events in Cornwall, beginning with his conception at Tintagel, that were told probably to interest or flatter the new earl of Cornwall from whom Geoffrey might have hoped for patronage. So what about those 'British treatises'?

The history of the Dark Ages is found rather by the spade than by the written word, but Gildas, a British monk writing in the 530s or 540s, was surely known to Geoffrey. In truth his book *De Excidio Britanniae* (Concerning the Fall of Britain) is less a history than a political sermon, denouncing the British leaders of his own time. It is his explanation of how the Britain he loves has come to be the object of Saxon invasion.

The Saxons came by invitation of the British ruler known as the high king, later named as Vortigern, to help him fight the

Picts. Having helped they stayed, made demands, revolted and ravaged the countryside as far as the western sea. They were permitted to remain in some defined areas but a British counter-attack was mounted by Ambrosius Aurelianus. For a time there was warfare ending in the British victory at Mount Badon about the year 500. The successors of Ambrosius in his own day fought amongst themselves, and the great victory was likely to be thrown away.

> Gildas has nothing to say of Arthur … the silence … may suggest that the Arthur of history was a less imposing figure than the Arthur of legend. But it should not be allowed to remove him from the sphere of history.
> Sir Frank Stenton, historian

Gildas only names Ambrosius as a leader immediately before his own time; he does not mention the victor at Badon, though later writers, of course, say it was Arthur. Perhaps the name is deliberately not used because it was so well known to his

The twelve battles of Arthur listed by 'Nennius', early 9th century.

readers. Gildas's story in general certainly rings true. He himself appears in later stories, both Welsh and English: a member of Arthur's court, a maker of peace between Arthur and Melwas, king of Somerset. And in death he belongs to Brittany where his body lies at St Gildas de Rhuys.

Later than Gildas, further from the time it records, but steeped in a tradition that points to south-east Wales, is a complex source often called Nennius (from a possible author Ninnius) and by some *Historia Brittonum* (History of the Britons). In its present form it dates from the early 9th century and in one chapter it lists twelve battles won by Arthur against the Saxons, the last at Badon, the list perhaps taken from a lost (and therefore possibly much earlier) Welsh poem.

And Welsh, too, are the *Annales Cambriae* (Annals of Wales), a 10th-century Latin chronicle, a table of 533 years, the first perhaps the year 447. Under Year 72 (518) the Battle of Badon was fought, 'in which Arthur carried the cross of Our Lord Jesus Christ on his shoulders for three days and three nights, and the Britons were victorious'. The word 'shoulders' might mean shield, and the cross an emblem or a relic. Either way a Christian king. And twenty-one years later 'the strife of Camlann, in which Arthur and Medraut (Mordred) fell'. There is much in Nennius that is fanciful or politically biassed, but the Welsh Annals tell otherwise of real, historical people, so why not Arthur?

The battle of Badon recorded in the Annals of Wales. 10th century.

> *I think we can dispose of him [Arthur] quite briefly. He owes his place in our history books to a 'no smoke without fire' school of thought.*
> Dr David Dumville

But there is another 'British treatise', using British in its widest sense, that Geoffrey of Monmouth knew. It is the story of a 5th-century 'king of the Britons' mentioned in the Breton *Legend of St Goeznovius*. Written in 1019 by someone called William, it tells as an introduction to the saint's work in Brittany a story with elements of Gildas and Geoffrey that he claims to have taken from something much earlier, something he calls *Ystoria Britanica*. It is the story of Britain invaded by pagan Saxons, first called in by their own king, Vortigern.

Some time later, the great Arthur, King of the Britons, managed to clear them from Britain 'after many victories that he won gloriously in Britain and Gaul' though after his time they returned to persecute the Christian church during a time when there were 'many kings, Saxons and Britons, striving back and forth'. Many men [including Goeznovius] went to Brittany.

So William's Arthur occurs about the 460s, and the information that he fought in Gaul as well as in Britain adds something new and important, a British source not from Wales nor Cornwall but from Brittany itself. And this source speaks of one styled 'Riothamus' or 'King of the Britons' who in 468 crossed to Gaul with 12,000 troops, possibly to give the Roman government there help against the advancing Visigoths. In the event the Roman governor and the Visigoths together defeated Riothamus near Chateauroux but he moved on to Burgundy, where the story ends.

For some critics the name Riothamus is a problem; for others it is convincingly interpreted as 'supreme king', and evidently to contemporaries was synonymous with Arthur. The expedition to France which in later (English) writers seemed too implausible has from such early and Breton sources to be taken seriously.

The Tale Made Taller?

Geoffrey of Monmouth's work proved so popular that by the end of the 12th century it was known in France, Spain, Italy, Poland and Byzantium. Some two hundred copies of it still survive in Britain. The Nobel Laureate John Steinbeck, working on his translation of Malory in the 1950s, was thrilled to discover that in Italy interest in things Arthurian had been widespread from as early as 1100 among what were described as 'the people of the streets' as distinct from 'the people of

Arthur, Gawaine and other knights carved above a door, Modena cathedral, 1100-10.

Arthur in a mosaic in Otranto cathedral, about 1165.

Dunster from Carhampton, Somerset.

the castles'. Carvings of Arthur, Gawaine and other knights over a doorway at Modena cathedral and a mosaic in Otranto cathedral would have expected their work to be recognised by passers by.

From the 12th century onwards readers of Geoffrey of Monmouth added significant elements and their own, not always consistent, versions of the story. Camelot was introduced by the French romantic writer Chretien de Troyes, the Round Table by the Norman known as Wace. The author of the Life of St Carannog made him a junior king at Dunster who had trouble with a dragon. In the Life of St Gildas Arthur was the man whose wife was held on Glastonbury Tor, the stronghold of Melwas, king of Somerset. For the 14th-century Glastonbury chronicler he was the king who sent the young man Yder to fight giants on what became their estate at Brent Knoll.

Glastonbury Tor, Somerset.

Brent Knoll, Somerset.

Glastonbury abbey, Lady Chapel.

The Arthurian connection with Glastonbury had by then become immensely important, for bones discovered in 1190/1 in the monks' graveyard there, an event carefully authenticated by several witnesses, identified Glastonbury as the Isle of Avalon. 'Here lies King Arthur on the Isle of Avalon' read the words on a cross in the grave. The political significance of the discovery was made plain when Edward I and Queen Eleanor took an active part in the ceremonial reburial of most of the bones of Arthur and Guinevere in a shrine in the newly-completed choir of the abbey church. The same king presided at a tournament at Winchester in 1290 when the centrepiece was the Round Table that still hangs on the wall in the castle there. That same king, who thought to add Scotland to his empire, was happy to look back to an earlier conqueror as his example.

The Arthurian shrine at Glastonbury in 1278 must be assumed to have attracted a steady stream of visitors and the abbey guide book known as the *Magna Tabula* created by

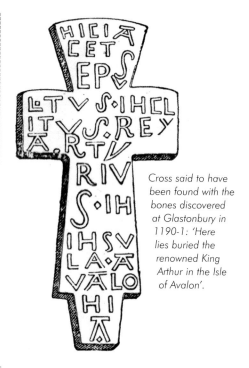

Cross said to have been found with the bones discovered at Glastonbury in 1190-1: 'Here lies buried the renowned King Arthur in the Isle of Avalon'.

The Round Table, Winchester.

Abbot Chinnock at the end of the 14th century elaborates the story of its creation. A rare surviving account roll of 1446-7 records that the abbey's sacrist was paid two shillings by the abbey's almoner for 'scouring' the tomb. In the 1530s John Leland, Henry VIII's antiquary, described a monument with inscriptions, a sword and a cross, perhaps an elaboration of the earlier tomb implied by the comment of a contemporary that the monks had 'not many years since … extruded a magnificent sepulture'. The cult of Arthur continued to Glastonbury's end. One of the monks to be hanged on the Tor with Abbot Whiting in 1539 was John Thorne who on joining the community many years before had become John Arthur.

Leland was also responsible for a significant identification. At South Cadbury, a few miles south of Glastonbury, he found

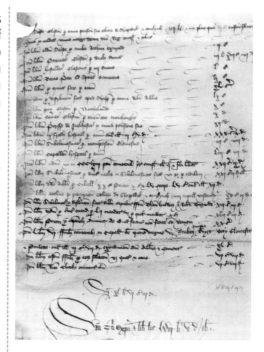

> 'Paid to the same Sacrist for scouring the tomb of Arthur, 2s' from the account roll (line 3) of the Glastonbury almoner, 1446-7.

'Camallate, sumtyme a famose toun or castelle ... the people ... have hard say that Arture much resorted to Camalat'. The site, he went on to say, had belonged to 'the old Lord Hungerford' and was in his time owned by 'Hastinges the Erle of Huntendune by his mother'. That same earl's grandson was later to write of the 'gallante hil where there hathe bene a castel in times past called Camelot, wherin Sir Lancelot in King Arthur's time is fayned to have dwelled'. But is there some heritage-creation here? Leland knew of the site's archaeological significance: Roman coins, found there, and more recently a silver horse-shoe; but the Hastings connection took ownership back to the son of that stalwart supporter of Edward IV William Hastings, Lord Hastings, whom Richard III summarily executed in 1483 lest he asked awkward questions about the king's nephews. The Arthurian Legend was still capable of development for private or for political purposes.

The Glastonbury Chair inscribed 'Johanes Arthurus monachus Glastone ... '

The 'castle' at South Cadbury, Somerset.

John Leland made notes on Arthurian sites in Gloucestershire, Cornwall and Wales as well as Somerset and there seems no end to sites there, Scotland, the North of England and Brittany that have found their enthusiastic, not to say fanatical identifiers since his time. The Round Table has been claimed in the Roman earthworks at Caerleon and many other places, and Arthur's seats, bridges, stones, tables, chairs and quoits have been named and almost venerated in folklore. His name is linked with sites of friend and foe alike, his tomb claimed, apart from Glastonbury, for at least two caves in Norway. And his spirit? In a cave beneath the site of Leland's Camelot Arthur and his knights lie sleeping. They are ready, when their country needs them, to rise again and fight as they did of old.

Excavations on the hill top at South Cadbury in the 1960s caused much archaeological and media excitement. The natural stronghold had been known to Bronze-Age people, made even stronger in the Iron Age, but not strong enough to withstand a Roman onslaught. Then later came men who rebuilt the defences to face another foe and left behind them traces of a great wooden hall and, more significant, the remains of earthenware vessels from the Mediterranean, once holding luxuries that only men of wealth and status could afford. Here, surely, was a site where a British leader might have stood to defend his region from an enemy advancing from the east or a base from which to fight twelve battles.

> *There would be a day – there must be a day – when he would come back to Gramarye with a new Round Table.*
> T.H. White, *The Once and Future King*.

Royal Attraction

Successive kings of England found the idea of King Arthur and his knights of political value. Henry II, claiming effective control of Wales, listened to the tales of a Welsh Bard who is said to have revealed that the king was buried at Glastonbury, though the discovery of his bones, first announced in Wales, was apparently made entirely by accident and was not the result of a serious search. Richard I, with wider interests, gave a sword said to have been Arthur's sword Excalibur to his ally Tancred of Sicily (how he came by it was never explained), and, perhaps part of a plan to embrace Brittany in his empire designated as his heir its prince, named Arthur. King John, caring neither for a rival nor for the name, had the young boy murdered; another Arthurian tragedy.

John's grandson Edward I has been described as an Arthurian enthusiast, clearly associated with the shrine at Glastonbury and the Round Table at Winchester.

Edward III, an empire-builder like his grandfather, formed in his Order of the Garter a mirror-image of the fellowship of the Round Table, the focus of a glittering court with the conquest of France as its holy grail. Tournaments took the place of real victories in Richard II's reign but Arthurian literature continued to proliferate among the chattering classes on both sides of the growing political divide that ended in the Wars of the Roses. A Yorkshire gentleman, Robert Thornton, who copied a poem entitled *Morte Arthure* written between 1399 and 1402, was obviously one of many enthusiasts for the story. Among others were Humphrey, duke of Gloucester, Henry V's brother, whose illegitimate son was named Arthur; and Humphrey's brother John, duke of Bedford, some of whose collection of Arthurian books from the

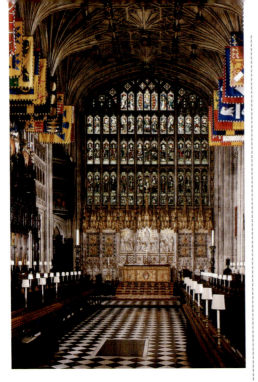

French royal library found their way to the Woodvilles. The figure of Arthur in stained glass in the choir of York Minster and in St Mary's Hall, Coventry, emulated royal interest.

With the arrival of Edward IV as king in 1461, royal propagandists had to give cover to his conquest by demonstrating an ancestry more satisfactory than that of his Lancastrian predecessor Henry VI. Arthur would not quite do for he had no legitimate son, but Uther Pendragon could take the line back to Brutus, and Cadwallader could embrace any Welsh doubts. Arthurian glory and chivalry could be demonstrated in London pageants and the king's own physical beauty; and the king's virility was proven in the appearance of an illegitimate son

*Left: St George's chapel, Windsor:
the Garter Knights' stalls and banners.*

*Opposite: 'King Arthur' on the Round Table,
re-painted by order of Henry VIII in 1516.*

named Arthur. And where the royal court went, others would follow.

The decline of great Yorkist promise was equally Arthurian, but Henry Tudor faced the same challenge, producing by Elizabeth of York a first son whom he named Arthur. And it was in the fateful year that Henry came to power, 1485, that Caxton produced what came to be the inspiration and solid foundation of all subsequent Arthurian literature in England. Sir Thomas Malory's work had been written during the worst crisis of Edward IV's reign, but no doubt long contemplated. His period of imprisonment in the 1450s during the Lancastrian regime was followed by fighting for, and relaxing at, tournaments with leading Yorkists, but he was a loose cannon. His friendship with members of the Neville family might have been the inspiration for the introduction of the names Arthur and Lancelot into their family, but his tendency towards lawlessness found him in gaol at the end of his life where his political friends may have provided him with the sources for his literary masterpiece, which he completed in 1469-70.

Arthur, Henry Tudor's eldest son, was born in 1486 and until his early death in 1502 was the fond hope of the new regime, as much dependent on propaganda as the Yorkists had been. His brother Henry's European ambitions and need for an ancestry to match those of his rival Francis I of France and the Emperor Charles V seem to have led to a repainting of the Round Table in 1516 to provide the figure of Arthur with the unmistakeable features of King Henry VIII. A few years later, displays of Arthurian and other pageantry in London and in France for the perusal of the two monarchs declared graphically what Henry and his subjects needed to believe: that only the English king's support for either side could bring victory. In the event, the need for a male heir to create a future for all this claimed ancestry gave rise to the English Reformation and Tudor isolation. Arthur was not called in aid of political support again.

Ignored by Shakespeare

John Leland was clearly passionate about King Arthur, absolutely convinced of his existence as a figure of history. He had seen so many books in monastic and other libraries during his search for books for Henry VIII, he had heard the Somerset folk-tales about Camelot and, perhaps his strongest argument, he had seen the king's seal at the shrine of Edward the Confessor at Westminster and had been overwhelmed with emotion: 'so great is both the majesty and the antiquity of the thing'. The seal had been one of the factors that persuaded Caxton to print Malory's work. Altogether, Leland became the leading Arthurian of his day and in 1544 published a book called *Assertio Inclytissimi Arturii Regis Britanniae*. Originally in Latin and thus not popularly accessible, it was translated in 1582 by Ralph Robinson as *A Worthy Assertion of Arthur King of Britain* and was dedicated to 'The Society of Archers in London, yearly celebrating the magnificence of Prince Arthur'. The king had become a prince, the knight a humble archer's icon. Other contemporary Arthurian works were equally minor including ballads and plays, perhaps the best *The Misfortunes of Arthur*, written by Thomas Hughes in 1588. The title hardly suggests a hero.

However 'terrible and formidable' the name of Arthur might have been to the chronicler Edward Hall when writing about the naming of Henry VII's heir, neither the name nor Edward Hall's opinion encouraged William Shakespeare to take him up. Perhaps *King Lear* was enough. There were sufficient tragedies from the 1530s not to want to relive them too often. The Emperor's ambassador declared in 1533 when Henry VIII had repudiated Katherine of Aragon that 'all that know the King have great pity at his misordering, considering his great nobleness and fame, which is greater than that of any prince since King Arthur'.

Elizabeth's throne was never entirely secure as a result of that misordering, but the flattering entertainment given the queen by the earl of Leicester at Kenilworth in 1575 began with a welcome by 'Arthurian giants' who spoke to her of the surrounding lake as originating in Arthur's time. Later in the programme came a song based on that challenge to the young Arthur by King Ryence of Northgalis for his beard. A welcome and a song; Arthur's role as a small part of a great entertainment is almost a tragedy in itself.

But Arthur was not entirely forgotten by another royal flatterer. Dr John Dee intrigued the queen by his suggestion that, as the undoubted descendant of the king, she should emulate his imperial power. Conquering France might, at the time, have been a less likely enterprise than in the time of Edward III, but Arthur had been accepted as overlord of Norway, so why not take over the whole of Scandinavia and even parts of Russia?

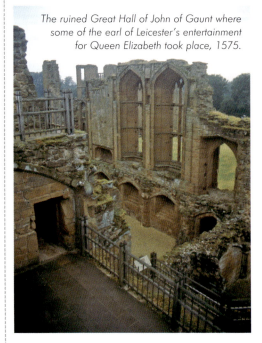

The ruined Great Hall of John of Gaunt where some of the earl of Leicester's entertainment for Queen Elizabeth took place, 1575.

From tragedy to fantasy to poetry. Philip Sidney thought about an Arthurian work but never achieved it; Edmund Spenser gave Arthur a part in *The Faerie Queene*, retelling his story before kingship was thrust upon him as a brave knight full of moral virtues 'most fit for the excellency of his person, being made famous by many men's former works'. The quotation, in his explanatory letter to Sir Walter Raleigh, makes clear the author's belief that Arthur was entirely fictional; and the title of the work betrays his real purpose: it was but a vehicle to achieve a place at court. And there was a clear political theme, for Arthur's chief adventures are the slaying of the three-bodied monster Gerioneo (Philp II of Spain), the rescue from him of Belge (the Netherlands) and the slaying of the Soudan in his 'chariot high' (Philip II and the Armada). Arthur might just be the earl of Leicester.

A knight from Edmund Spenser's Faerie Queene, *1590.*

Avalon praised and pictured: Michael Drayton, Polyolbion, *1622.*

✲ The Argvment.

In this third Song, great threatnings are,
And tending all to Nymphiſh warre.
Old Wanſdike *vttereth words of hate,*
Deprauing Stonendges *eſtate.*
Cleere Avon *and faire* Willy *ſtriue,*
Each pleading her prerogatiue.
The Plaine *the* Forreſts *doth diſdaine:*
The Forreſts *raile vpon the* Plaine.
The Muſe then ſeekes the Shires extreames,
To find the Fountaine of great Tames;
Falls downe with Avon, *and diſcries*
Both Bathes *and* Briſtowes *braueries:*
Then viewes the Sommerſetian *ſoyle;*
Through Marſhes, Mines, *and* Mores *doth toyle,*
To Avalon *to* Arthurs *Graue,*
Sadlie bemoan'd of Ochy Caue.
Then with delight ſhee brauelie brings
The Princely Parret *from her Springs:*
Preparing for the learned Plea
(The next Song) in the Seuerne *Sea.*

Arthur was given passing appearances in court masques in James I's early years, in Ben Jonson's *The Speeches at Prince Henry's Barriers* (1610) speaking with Merlin in praise of recent English monarchs; and a gradually increasing awareness of topography inspired Michael Drayton to embark on a poetic description of Britain entitled *Polyolbion*, completed in 1622. It included Arthur's seat and the Round Table at Winchester, his tomb with that of 'holy Joseph' at Glastonbury, and other seats at Caerleon and Camelot near the River Brue. The rivers of Wales, Drayton declared, sang the glories of Arthur, the Severn recalled the prophecies of Merlin. All decidedly poetic, of course, and inspired, in a sense, by the re-creation of the concept of Britain in the union of the crowns of England and Scotland on the accession of King James.

A more sober voice was added to Drayton's text in the form of 'illustrations' or historical commentaries contributed by his friend the lawyer-antiquarian John Selden. Selden's great knowledge of early historical sources led him to doubt the existence of an historical Arthur, a view that was close to his political opinions about kings claiming divine powers. Obviously he had no wish to offend his friend and blamed not him but 'poetical monks' and their 'intermixed and absurd fauxities' that had allowed people to believe such unhistorical events. Yet there was clearly something about the earthworks at South Cadbury that could not be gainsaid. Far less substantial was the first appearance about 1620 of Tom Thumb, Arthur's dwarf, and of ballads providing the basis for children's stories and songs. How far the hero king had fallen!

The political opinions that put Selden against the autocratic pretensions of the Stuart kings prevented John Milton from writing the epic he planned, telling of Britons colonising Armorica, of the birth of Arthur, and of Britons at war. His time and energy were taken up with pamphleteering against Crown oppression, and the epic he finally wrote after serving Cromwell so faithfully was *Paradise Lost*. Milton had become a revolutionary, not interested in any sort of glorious past with 'fabled knights in battles feigned' or 'gorgeous knights at joust or tournament'. And the cause he had believed in had itself been lost. The king he had helped to remove had been replaced by another king.

But in time, and Milton would surely have rejoiced, the people managed to limit the powers of the king, and the politics of party permeated deep. Scholars following Selden looked to the past to justify their views as perhaps never before, and poets were divided on both party and religious lines. King Arthur found a supporter in Sir Richard Blackmore, rather better known as physician to King William III than a poet, who determined, nevertheless to write the epic Milton had once planned and John Dryden was even then contemplating. Meanwhile, in 1691 Dryden wrote the libretto for an opera called *King Arthur: or, The British Worthy* for which Henry Purcell contributed rather disappointing music. Blackmore's *Prince Arthur: An Heroick Poem in Ten Books* appeared in 1695 and *King Arthur* in 1697. They owed much to Geoffrey of Monmouth as far as its historical content was concerned, and Spenser and Milton were his poetic mentors, but typical of his own time with its acute religious differences, Blackmore saw Arthur as the champion of Protestantism as opposed to the Catholic Jacobites, the adherents of the exiled Stuarts, and their dubiously loyal co-religionists. Much to the annoyance of the country's real poet at the time, John Dryden, Blackmore's epic far outshone the opera and was a huge popular success. Alexander Pope consigned Blackmore to his *Dunciad* as 'the Everlasting Blackmore', partly for writing so much, and his real offence, both for Pope and for Dryden, his attack on their religious beliefs.

> *Who Arthur was, and whether ever any such reigned in Britain, hath been doubted heretofore, and may again with good reason.*
> John Milton

The Return of Romance

The Grand Tour and the consequent interest in Classical studies dominated the literary and architectural scene for most of the 18th century, but the beginning of serious professional interest in the historical resources of the state led to the re-emergence of an increasing interest in the Middle Ages and its heroes. Earlier in the 18th century, at the hands of Henry Fielding, the Tom Thumb theme was revived, rather to make fun of contemporary playwrights by way of a love triangle involving Arthur, the Queen of the Giants, Arthur's daughter Huncamunca and Tom Thumb himself. Thomas Percy's *Reliques of Ancient English Poetry* (1765) revived interest in Arthurian texts and Thomas Warton in his *History of English Poetry* (1774-81) did the same. Malory's *Morte D'Arthur,* not published since 1634, re-appeared in 1816.

So Arthurian literature began to be taken seriously alongside the growing interest in historic sources. Arthur became respectable again but the great early Romantic poets such as Shelley, Keats and Byron, like Shakespeare before them, were curiously indifferent. Sir Walter Scott, William Wordsworth and Thomas Love Peacock all used Arthurian themes or characters, but Arthur's real saviour was Alfred, Lord Tennyson. He found a copy of Malory in his father's library and began work on the theme in 1830. *Idylls of the King* was finally completed in 1885, a clear antidote to the materialism of the age, condemning illicit love but accepting the inevitable destruction of Arthur's world at his death.

Poets after Tennyson — in the 19th century Bulwer-Lytton, Ernest Rhys, Matthew Arnold and A.C. Swinburne, in the 20th T.S. Eliot, John Masefield and Charles Williams — took up Arthurian themes in differing ways, but they were overtaken in

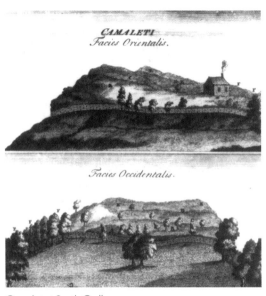

Camelot at South Cadbury.

Right: A nineteenth-century interpretation of Arthurian legend. Aubrey Beardsley

volume if not in quality by novelists and dramatists, librettists, scriptwriters and cartoonists. And running alongside them were graphic artists from the Pre-Raphaelites onwards, notably Holman Hunt, D.G. Rossetti, Edward Burne-Jones, Gustave Dore and Aubrey Beardsley; and the composer Richard Wagner with his Arthurian works *Tristan und Isolde* (1865) and *Parsifal* (1882) that found their 20th-century counterpart in the musical *Camelot* (1960), libretto by Alan Jay Lerner and score by Frederick Loewe, based on T.H.White's *The Once and Future King* (1958). Has ever a king inspired so much art?

If there is no historical truth in a story told over fifteen centuries, then its survival is truly remarkable. The long-standing truths of Jesus and Buddha, for John Steinbeck, were in the same mould: elaborated by some, confirmed by others but remaining resolutely held with a passion by generations. Heroic and tragic by turns but surviving apparent failure to be waited for in triumph.

... the myth of Arthur continues even into the present day and is an inherent part of the so-called 'Western' with which television is filled at the present time – same characters, same methods, same stories, only slightly different weapons and certainly different topography. But if you change Indians or outlaws for Saxons and Picts and Danes, you have exactly the same story.
John Steinbeck

Left: *Glastonbury Tor.*

Opposite: *Merlin taking the child Arthur into his keeping. Aubrey Beardsley.*

Further Reading

Richard Barber (ed.), *The Arthurian Legends: An Illustrated Anthology,* The Boydell Press, 1979

Richard Barber, *King Arthur: Hero and Legend,* The Boydell Press, 1986

Martin Biddle, *King Arthur's Round Table,* The Boydell Press, 2000

N.J. Higham, *King Arthur: Myth-Making and History,* Routledge, 2002

Jonathan Hughes, *Arthurian Myths and Alchemy: The Kingship of Edward IV,* Sutton Publishing, 2002

Elizabeth Jenkins, *The Mystery of King Arthur,* Michael Joseph, 1975

Norris J. Lacy and Geoffrey Ashe with Debra N. Mancoff, *The Arthurian Handbook,* Garland Publishing Inc., 1997

Sir Thomas Malory, *Le Morte D'Arthur,* Omega Books, 1985

Geoffrey of Monmouth, *The History of the Kings of Britain,* translated by Lewis Thorpe, Folio Society, 1969

C.A. Ralegh Radford and Michael J. Swanton, *Arthurian Sites in the West,* Univ. of Exeter Press, 2002

John Steinbeck, *The Acts of King Arthur and his Noble Knights,* ed. Chase Horton, Book Club Associates, 1977

L Alcock, *By South Cadbury is that Camelot ...,* Thames and Hudson, 1972